2.95

D0591326

THE ANAYA **SUN SIGN** *COMPANIONS*

VIRGO

24 August-23 September

CELESTINE O'RYAN

ANAYA PUBLISHERS LIMITED
LONDON

First published in Great Britain in 1991 by
Anaya Publishers Ltd., Strode House, 44-50 Osnaburgh Street, London NW1 3ND

Copyright © Anaya Publishers Ltd 1991

ASTROLOGICAL CONSULTANT Jan Kurrels

Managing Editor	Judy Martin
Art Director	Nigel Osborne
Designers	Sally Stockwell
	Anne Clue
Illustrators	Marion Appleton
	David Ashby
	Lorraine Harrison
	Tony Masero
Indexer	Peter Barber

All rights reserved.
No part of this publication may be reproduced, stored
in a retrieval system, or transmitted, in any form or
by any means, electronic, mechanical, photocopying,
recording or otherwise, without the permission of the
copyright holder.

British Library Cataloguing in Publication Data
O'Ryan, Celestine
    Virgo. – (Anaya sun sign companions).
    1. Astrology
    I. Title
    133.52
    ISBN 1-85470-095-2

TYPESET IN GREAT BRITAIN BY MIDFORD TYPESETTING LTD, LONDON
COLOUR ORIGINATION IN SINGAPORE BY COLUMBIA OFFSET LTD
PRINTED IN SINGAPORE BY TIMES OFFSET LTD

CONTENTS

VIRGO

Most people know their own sun sign, and you know that yours is Virgo, but do you appreciate its full impact on every area of your life? Your Sun Sign Companion *is a guide to the many pleasures and preferences that are specific to you as a Virgoan subject.*

Your personality profile is here – and much more. You can find out not only where you fit into the grand astrological scheme and the ways the other zodiac signs connect with your own, but also discover the delights of the Virgoan foods that are your special delicacies; the plants that you should grow in your garden to enhance your Virgoan moods; the animals that you appreciate for their affinities to your sign and the pets that you as a Virgo can easily love and live with; the ways in which you need to take care of your body, and how your health and well-being may be affected by the fact that you were born under Virgo.

The fascinating range of this Sun Sign Companion *explains your temperament, your actions and the ways you live your life in zodiacal terms. You are practical and hard working and your special element – Virgoan earth – makes you creative and dependable; your planetary ruler Mercury, the messenger of the gods, encourages your resourcefulness. You have singular connections with the powers of the Earth itself – its gemstones, metals and crystals. And your zodiacal profile is underlined by your Virgoan connections to the ancient and mysterious arts of the Runes and the Tarot.*

This book provides you with the intriguing mosaic of influences, interests and attributes that build into the total picture of yourself as a Virgoan. More than any other zodiacal guide, your Sun Sign Companion *reveals to you the inherent fun and enjoyment of life under Virgo.*

THE ZODIAC

hen the ancient astrologers studied the sky at night, they tracked the obvious motion and changing shape of the Moon, but noted two other phenomena: the frosty grandeur of the fixed stars and the different movements of the five observable planets. Mercury, Venus, Mars, Jupiter and Saturn moved and weaved about the night sky in repeating patterns, always within the same narrow strip of the heavens. And in the day time, the Sun could be seen progressing along the centre of this strip on its apparent orbit. Most of the action, celestially speaking, appeared to take place in a restricted

heavenly corridor. Astronomers and astrologers therefore gave priority to this ribbon of sky, and noted what else appeared in it.

Sharing the strip were twelve fixed star constellations, known from ancient times. They were Aries the Ram, Taurus the Bull, Gemini the Twins, Cancer the Crab, Leo the Lion, Virgo the Virgin, Libra the Balance, Scorpius the Scorpion, Sagittarius the Archer, Capricornus the Goat, Aquarius the Water Carrier and Pisces the Fishes. As most of the constellations are named after sentient creatures, the Greeks called this band of sky the zodiac, from their word meaning images of animals or living beings.

In astronomical terms, the constellations take up varying amounts of sky and exhibit different degrees of brightness. Astrologically, they are assigned equal prominence and importance, and are given equal 30-degree arcs of the celestial band. These are the signs of the zodiac, and the starting point on the celestial circle is 0 degrees Aries, which was the point of the vernal equinox over 4000 years ago when the zodiac was established.

The celestial jostling along the zodiacal corridor is explained by the fact that the planets orbit the Sun roughly in the same plane. Imagine yourself at the centre of a race track, timing a group of runners as they lap the circuit, each one running at a different pace and in a different lane. Soon you would be able to predict when each one would pass you, especially if you noted down landmarks along the spectator stands behind the runners.

In the same way, astrologers pinpoint the position and motion of any planet, using the zodiac band as a reference grid. Interpretation of the effects of planetary power filtered through the zodiac grid is the enduring fascination of astrology. The planets are extremely powerful, as represented by their having been awarded the names and attributes of the gods.

ZODIACAL INFLUENCES

our sun sign is the zodiac sign that the Sun, the most powerful of the heavenly bodies, appears to be passing through from our viewpoint on Earth at the time of your birth. It takes the Sun one year to progress through all the signs, and it is the Sun's huge power, filtered through each sign in turn, that etches the broad character templates of the signs. Over the centuries, each sign has acquired its own repertory of characteristics and personality traits, a seamless blend of archetypal myth and particular observation. So now we can talk about, say, a 'typical Virgo' with the expectation that others will know what we mean. However, fine tuning and modification of the individual personality are dictated by two conditions at the time of birth – the positions of the Moon and planets in the zodiac and the nature of the ascendant, the sign rising on the eastern horizon at the moment of birth.

The Earth spins counter-clockwise daily on its axis, but to us it appears that the Sun, stars and planets wheel overhead from east to west. Within this framework, the zodiac passing overhead carries with it one sign every two hours; therefore the degree of the ascendant changes likewise, which explains why two people born on the same day can have such varying personalities. The influence of the ascending sign, and any planet positioned in it, has a strong bearing on the formation of the personality. A Virgoan with Pisces in the ascendant is quite a different kettle of fish to one with Capricorn ascending.

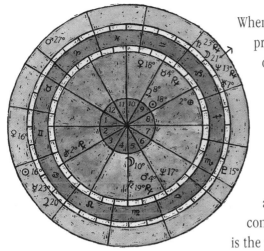

When an astrologer prepares a birth chart, or horoscope, for an individual, it is a two-dimensional record of these three-dimensional events in the heavens, represented graphically as a wheel encompassing concentric rings. The Earth is the pinpoint at the centre of the wheel and is surrounded by twelve fixed segments representing the zodiacal Houses, the areas of life in which planetary influences will manifest themselves. The outer circle of the chart represents the moving zodiacal corridor, divided into its twelve segments – the signs of the zodiac.

The predictability of the planets' movements has enabled astrologers to create tables, known as Ephemerides, of the planetary positions past, present and future. Once the positions of the Sun, Moon and planets have been established for a specific time, and a particular subject, the astrologer can assess and interpret what effects the planets will have, how they will enhance, diminish or frustrate each other's powers, and which areas of the subject's life will come under their particular influences. And all of this information is blended with the astrologer's understanding of the sun sign personality, the broad framework of individuality in zodiacal terms.

THE VIRGO PERSONALITY

 irgo is the sixth sign of the zodiac. Meticulous, methodical, practical and precise, Virgo is intrigued by the details and dynamics of the many kinds of system that silently govern the world, from bus timetables to grand philosophical theories. Virgoans work hard to break down the systems into comprehensible pieces, focusing on the pattern rather than the grand design. Sometimes their fascination with detail can blind them to the wider scheme of things: they are often unable to see the wood for the trees.

Obsession with detail can lead Virgos to become set in their ways, especially when it comes to health, diet and hygiene. The practical, helpful, organized friend can dwindle into an unendearing fusspot, nit-picking and hypercritical of any non-Virgoan approaches to life (or to cleaning the bathroom). Coupled with Virgo's natural modesty and reticence, this critical attitude can make Virgoans appear cold and stand-offish, blighting friendships and love affairs; then poor Virgo pines wretchedly.

Being subject to Mercury, Virgo is restless, like its brother sign Gemini, but less flighty: this is an earth sign, after all. Undissipated nervous energy can cause illness, and Virgo solves the problem by keeping busy, filling the unforgiving hours not spent at work with useful activities and worthy hobbies. For Virgo truly believes that the devil makes work for idle hands; the Mercury who rules this sign is herald of the underworld as well as messenger of the gods.

Uirgo
Orbis Regens
Mercurius
Signum Obstans
Pisces

THE PLANETARY RULER

 ncient astrologers named the five planets they could see in the night sky after the five most powerful classical gods; naturally, the planets took on the attributes and associations of the gods, and a pleasingly symmetrical system was devised to distribute this planetary power throughout the zodiac.

The Sun and Moon, being the most dazzling lights, ruled one sun sign each (Leo and Cancer). The remaining ten signs managed under the shared patronage of the five planets. Mercury presided over Gemini and Virgo, Venus over Taurus and Libra, Mars over Aries and Scorpio, Jupiter over Sagittarius and Pisces, and Saturn over Aquarius and Capricorn.

When more planets were discovered after the invention of the telescope in 1610, a reshuffle became necessary. Uranus

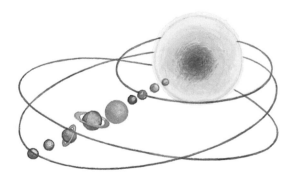

(discovered in 1781) was allocated to Aquarius, Neptune (1836) was thought appropriate for Pisces, and Pluto (1930) now broods over Scorpio. This has unbalanced the symmetry: the search is on for other planets to share the burden with Venus and Mercury. Indeed, the asteroid Chiron, discovered in 1977 looping the void between Saturn and Uranus, is considered by some astrologers to

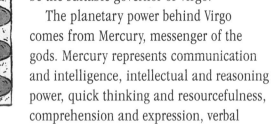

be the suitable governor of Virgo.

The planetary power behind Virgo comes from Mercury, messenger of the gods. Mercury represents communication and intelligence, intellectual and reasoning power, quick thinking and resourcefulness, comprehension and expression, verbal skills and cerebral fancy. It is versatile, lively, playful and curious. Adversely, it can produce chronic restlessness, inconsistency, nerviness, inquisitiveness and an addiction to low cunning.

Astronomically, Mercury the Messenger is the innermost planet of the solar system. Dense and small (it would almost be lost in the Atlantic Ocean), it dashes around the Sun once every eighty-eight days, and may stay a few days or a few weeks in each zodiac sign. It is so close to the Sun that its vigorous twinkle is often outshone – it can occasionally be seen in the east just before sunrise and in the west around dusk.

In classical mythology, Mercury was the messenger of the gods, the Roman equivalent of the Greek Hermes, who is the patron of medicine, bearer of the *caduceus*, the staff of intertwined serpents that is the universal trademark of the medical profession today.

V I R G O

PATTERNS IN THE STARS

tar pictures, or images of the constellations, are in the eye of the beholder. What we see as a neighbourly cluster is usually an optical illusion, the stars in the group being many light years apart. Even so, the urge to impose a friendly pattern on the frosty grandeur of the night sky, to link the stars with the myths and legends on Earth, has been irresistible to all cultures. Different cultures make out different pictures, and the results are sometimes inscrutable – searching for Leo, say, you will look in vain for the shape of a lion pricked out in stars against the dark backcloth of the night sky.

The zodiac constellations were among the first to be made out, as they were the star groups that formed the background to the moving planets, and provided a useful reference grid to plot the planetary movements. In turn, they gave their names to the signs of the zodiac, although they spread unevenly across the sky and are not tidily confined to the equal 30-degree segments of the imaginary zodiac band. Many stars are known by their Arabic names, and the star that shone brightest when Arabic astrologers were compiling their star catalogues is designated its alpha.

The constellation that gave its name to the fifth sign of the zodiac is Virgo the Virgin, an enormous and resplendent star group that straddles the celestial equator. It is among the oldest and most important of the zodiac constellations. There are at least eleven bright stars visible to the naked eye and the alpha is the beautiful Spica, the sixteenth brightest star in the sky. Spica is the Latin word for ear of corn, a name that reflects Virgo's close association with the earth goddess Demeter.

Virgo also yields a rich harvest of galaxies, collectively known as the Virgo Cluster: twenty have been officially catalogued and hundreds more are known, although they are difficult to see without a very powerful telescope.

Virgo is the starry image of Astraea, an early goddess of justice and innocence. Daughter of Zeus and the Titaness Themis, Astraea attempted to inculcate sweet order and reason into humankind, but was so appalled by its unruly ungodliness that she resigned from the project and retired to the heavens. Virgo is also often equated with Demeter and her daughter Persephone.

THE ATTRACTION OF OPPOSITES

n astrological terms, polarity describes the strong complementary relationship between signs that are exactly opposite each other on the zodiac circle, 180 degrees or six signs apart. These signs share the same gender – masculine or feminine – and the same quality – cardinal, fixed or mutable – and so share the ways they look at the world and shape their energy. Characteristics and interests complement each other or harmonize on different scales.

Relationships between polar signs are often very satisfying and fruitful, especially in the context of work. A clue to this affinity lies with the elements governed by each sign. The mathematics of polarity mean that earth signs oppose only water signs, and that fire opposes only air. Fire and air signs therefore encourage and inspire each other – fire cannot burn without air and air needs heat to rise. Earth and water signs conspire together creatively – earth without water is unfruitful, water unconfined by earth wastes

its energy in diffusion – and together they make mud, rich material for any creative process.

Six signs away from neat, precise, methodical Virgo, the most organized sign in the zodiac, we find imaginative, water-borne Pisces, for whom anything is possible and classification is anathema. Imaginative, emotional Pisces – who has a time-share, if not a permanent lease, on property in the land of dreams – is surely guaranteed to cause frustration in practical, forward-planning Virgo, who lives life with both feet firmly on the ground.

Below the surface, however, a shared and complementary shaping energy is at work, the transforming energy of mutability. Both Virgo and Pisces preside over transitional times of the year, that space between the dissolution of the old season and the evolution of the new when all is exhilaratingly open to exploration. Virgo, the earth sign, watches over the transition from fruition to harvest in the Northern Hemisphere, and from seed-sowing to germination in the Southern. Pisces, the water sign, comes last in the order of the zodiac signs and holds the energies and dreams of the entire cycle in a sea of infinite potential, ready to begin all over again.

The complementary aspect of polarity is also seen in the characteristics traditionally associated with the two signs. Both are at their best when helping and healing. Virgo is associated with daily practicalities and making life run smoothly. Pisces's great gift for empathy cares for the world and its inhabitants on a spiritual plane.

THE SYMBOLS OF THE ZODIAC

ver since astrology began, there has been a kind of astrological shorthand, a set of symbols or ideograms called glyphs. Glyphs make the language of astrology universal and available to people who have no literary tradition. They also make it a lot easier to draw up a birth chart, being a convenient form of notation, especially where planets are clustered in one area of the chart.

Each of the zodiac signs has its own glyph, as do the planets. They have evolved over centuries, and so are now freighted with symbolism, not simply convenient codes.

Today, the glyph for Virgo is an M, with an elegant loop doubling over the last leg. Early Egyptians were more explicit, the Virgo hieroglyph being recognizably a seated, queenly woman, possibly a grain goddess adopted from Babylonian worship. The Greeks had two rather enigmatic

symbols, like freely drawn profiles of sitting figures. Medieval astrologers had two versions, neither a convincing prototype of the modern glyph; one is an upright cross with a banner waving bravely leftwards from the top of it; the other is an X-shaped cross, with the identical banner blowing from the top of the left-to-right diagonal.

There is a special fascination in studying the glyphs to see what other symbolism may be contained within them. The downward strokes of Virgo's M might represent the harrow that scours the earth after harvest or before seed sowing, the flourish at the end of the glyph referring to the ears of corn gathered at harvest time.

Planets also have their glyphs, and the Mercury symbol is rather complex, representing the male and female elements that are necessary for a fruitful harvest. The glyph is a circle mounted on a cross (like that for Venus); surmounting the circle is a semicircle, which is reminiscent both of Mercury's winged helmet and the horns that typically indicate maleness.

V I R G O

THE HOUSE OF VIRGO

he twelve Houses are an intellectual concept, not a physical reality, an expression of all the aspects of human life and experience, from the self to the infinite. Each is associated with a sign of the zodiac, sharing its planetary ruler and elemental energy. However, the Houses are fixed and constant – they are represented by the

central numbered segments on a birth chart – and the signs and planets pass through them. They are the channels through which planetary and zodiacal energies flow, and indicate which area of life is the focus of particular zodiacal influence at any one time.

Virgo, being the sixth sign of the zodiac, is associated with the Sixth House, which is also overseen by Virgo's planetary ruler, Mercury. Like Virgo, it is grounded in earth energy, and therefore concerns itself with material possessions and worldly circumstance. In particular, the Sixth House is concerned with physical work and how you organize your domestic life; and also with your physical health and how you look after your body – although this House is not entirely responsible for the constitution you are born with.

22

The Sixth House is a very orderly place, furnished with a
well-stocked medicine cabinet, somewhere to coordinate the
family timetable and file the endless lists and rotas that make
domestic life run smoothly.

When Mercury is in the Sixth House, it magnifies the Virgoan
tendency to fret about health matters and to allow minor problems
to loom out of all proportion.

ELEMENTS AND QUALITIES

I t was Aristotle, the great Greek thinker, who formalized the idea that all life is made up from infinitely various permutations of the four elements – fire, earth, air and water. In the zodiac cycle there are three signs representing each element. Aries, Leo and Sagittarius are for fire; Taurus, Virgo and Capricorn for earth; Gemini, Libra and Aquarius for air; and Cancer, Scorpio and Pisces for water.

However, in each case, the element is filtered through a different kind, or quality, of energy field; cardinal, fixed and mutable (or transforming). Aries, Cancer, Libra and Capricorn are cardinal; Taurus, Leo, Scorpio and Aquarius are fixed; Gemini, Virgo, Sagittarius and Pisces are mutable. Each sign is a unique manifestation of one element and one quality of energy.

Earth is the Virgo element: solid, dependable, full of infinite potential, the source of all nourishment, wealth and creativity. Fertile earth yields crops to feed us and our animals and produces the minerals and precious stones that we designate as riches. As clay, it is arguably the basis of civilization – how would we have progressed without cooking pots, storage jars, building bricks? Earth is mother, home, security, safety – witness the atavistic terror that seizes even the most sophisticated when they are caught up in an earthquake, which shakes life to its very foundation.

Virgo loves to see the earth at work, yielding up the bounty of its crops or neatly ploughed and harrowed ready to receive new seeds. Virgo understands that close attention to order and system are what keeps chaos at bay during times of transition and evolution. If the earth's harvest is not efficiently gathered and stored, or if there is no investment in new growth, famine and desolation will ensue.

Virgoan energy is mutable. Mutable energy people change the rules; they are the movers, transformers, changers, confidently releasing the potential of their particular energy. Virgoans oversee the orderly transformation of Earth, standing firm when sheets of golden wheat become fields of desolate brown stubble and are made ready to begin the cycle again, confident that their organizational skills will deliver the goods.

THE ZODIAC GARDEN

 ompetent at the wheel of an ecologically sound, lead-free-fuelled runabout, or bowling along busily on a big-wheeled bicycle, what Virgo likes to see is the countryside at work – the patchwork of fields a hive of rural industry, reassuringly large heaps of baled hay, great combines bringing in the sheaves, the rich earth being tilled and tended. Not that they despise the decorative: Virgoans appreciate small, neat, detailed flowers, especially blue and yellow ones. Particular attractions include the flowers of the cornfields and pasture lands: poppies, cornflowers, corn marigolds, yellow toadflax, cowslips, harebells, daisies. Modest woodland flowers – forget-me-nots, bluebells, primulas, periwinkles – also meet with Virgo's approval, but it is best if the plant is useful as well as beautiful; bright blue speedwell, also known as eyebright because it was a cure for sore eyes, or white and yellow feverfew, a remedy for headaches and fever.

In fact, all medicinal plants attract Virgoans: they will make room in their garden for any plant with *officinalis* (meaning for medicinal use) in its name. Ideally, Virgoans would grow what the medieval herbalists called a 'physick' garden; actually, they can make any garden grow.

Virgoan gardens are hard-working – no hothouse luxury for them. Most of the land will be given over to vegetables and herbs, grown in neat, orderly beds. Of course, these will be run on organic lines, with other plants providing the pesticides wherever possible – for example, the powerful scent from dill herb deals very effectively with bean pest. Virgoans sneer at conservatories: they have a proper greenhouse or potting shed, in which they spend hours potting on, pricking out, propagating rootstocks, sorting out seedlings and experimenting with the ideal proportions for the most effective growing mixture. If there is room for a flower garden, it will contain sensible plants such as the hypericum, Saint John's Wort, a rounded yellow border shrub with an impeccable history as a healing plant. A real Virgoan indulgence would be a camomile lawn, with flowers that bruise into purifying fragrance when walked upon.

A Virgo confined to houseplants would choose suitable food plants (tomatoes, avocados), herbs, or useful things such as the tobacco plant *Nicotiana*, which doubles as a fly repellent. In the long winter evenings, when all the gardening chores are done, Virgo will leaf through a pressed flower collection or embroider meticulous tapestries strewn with tiny, useful flowers.

V I R G O
ASTROLOGY AND THE ARK

he word zodiac derives from the Greek word for living creatures, and many of the signs are symbolized by animals. Virgo, however, is among the minority represented by the human figure, in this case the demure maiden, cool, calm and collected, rational and organized, seemingly poles apart from the instinctive, unpredictable lives led by animals.

Yet Virgo has a very strong bond with the animal kingdom. Virgo's ruler, Mercury, is almost overwhelmed with responsibilities as a god. One of these is the care of animals in general, specifically the herds and flocks which represented the triumph of human resourcefulness over the raw material of nature. Virgo itself is strongly associated with domestic animals of all kinds, from pets to working farm animals.

Any animal living with Virgo will be fortunate: properly nourished, appropriately housed, loved unsentimentally, and extremely well trained. In return for excellent treatment, Virgo expects the animal to make itself useful, earn its keep either by working or providing a useful product. To Virgo as the guardian of

the grain store, mice and rats are a real threat; therefore Virgo's self-possessed, sleek little tabby will be a ruthless mouser, and the well-tempered dog will be a great ratter.

Virgo will run a tight but happy ship on the smallholding or farm: the free-range ducks and chickens will be industrious layers, the rabbits in their immaculate hutches will breed – well, like rabbits. Stout-legged working horses, herds of contented dairy cows with methodically colour-coded ear tags, flocks of thick-fleeced sheep are what Virgo likes to see; but Virgo's favourite working animal has to be the sheepdog – intelligent, intuitive, discriminating and disciplined, the ultimate organizer of the animal world.

VIRGO ON THE MAP

Mundane astrology charts the birth of nations: countries, cities and major towns come under zodiacal influence, just as their inhabitants do. Often the ascendant, the sign in the First House which characterizes the nation as a whole, is more significant than the sun sign. Various methods are used to assess which zodiac sign holds sway where. Countries with an incontestable birthday – Christmas Day 1066, the day William the Conqueror was crowned king of England, for instance – have a standard birth chart. In countries which have evolved more organically, zodiacal influences may be deduced by the broad characteristics – can you think of a more suitable ruling sign than Taurus for Switzerland, the land loud with cowbells? Cities and towns may show their zodiac allegiance by their function – many ports come under the crusty care of water-loving Cancer, and the administrative heart of any capital city is ruled by Capricorn, the zodiac's bureaucrat.

Virgo's worldly subjects include Greece, Turkey, Mesopotamia, Brazil and the West Indies. Greece, Turkey and Mesopotamia radiate ancient power, and are the cradles of modern civilization. They oversaw social order born from anarchic chaos, and shaped the philosophical, political and cultural systems that form the basis of western public and intellectual life. Mesopotamia is the ancient name for Iraq and Syria, and the rest of the land between the rivers Tigris and Euphrates. Formerly called the 'fertile crescent', this was the ancient world's grain silo.

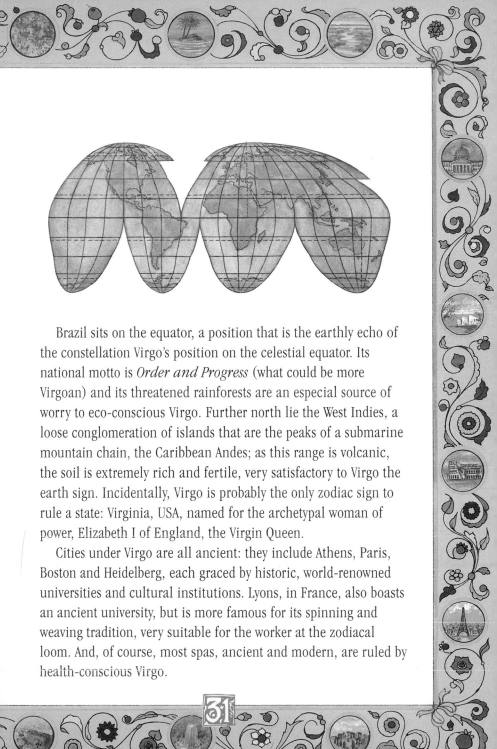

Brazil sits on the equator, a position that is the earthly echo of the constellation Virgo's position on the celestial equator. Its national motto is *Order and Progress* (what could be more Virgoan) and its threatened rainforests are an especial source of worry to eco-conscious Virgo. Further north lie the West Indies, a loose conglomeration of islands that are the peaks of a submarine mountain chain, the Caribbean Andes; as this range is volcanic, the soil is extremely rich and fertile, very satisfactory to Virgo the earth sign. Incidentally, Virgo is probably the only zodiac sign to rule a state: Virginia, USA, named for the archetypal woman of power, Elizabeth I of England, the Virgin Queen.

Cities under Virgo are all ancient: they include Athens, Paris, Boston and Heidelberg, each graced by historic, world-renowned universities and cultural institutions. Lyons, in France, also boasts an ancient university, but is more famous for its spinning and weaving tradition, very suitable for the worker at the zodiacal loom. And, of course, most spas, ancient and modern, are ruled by health-conscious Virgo.

EARTH'S BOUNTY

ood plants associated with Virgo are all the vegetables that grow below ground and all varieties of grain and cereals, foods deeply rooted in and dependent upon Virgo's home element, earth. The list provides pleasantly solid variety: carrots, radishes, turnips, parsnips, swedes, beetroot, celeriac, salsify, kohlrabi, jerusalem

artichokes. Like Gemini, Virgos also lay claim to the 'fruits' of nut-bearing trees, courtesy of their joint ruler Mercury – walnuts, hazelnuts, almonds, filberts, sweet chestnuts, pecans, pistachios, butternuts, brazil nuts, cashews and pine nuts.

Put them together and you have the basic ingredients for a healthy vegetarian diet; and the many herbs that Virgo rules add interest to vegetarian dishes. Vegetarianism suits Virgoans: their digestion is notoriously fragile, easily disturbed by anxiety and nervous upset; they need to nourish themselves well, avoiding rich food, keeping fat levels low and taking in lots of fibre. Virgo can cope well with a restricted or specialist diet, revelling in the careful planning and organization needed to avoid the vitamin deficiency (especially of the vitamin B complex) that can result from meatless eating.

The ideal Virgo kitchen would be traditional, earthy, rustic – hung about with dried herbs and strings of onions, the shelves winking with glass jars of pickles and preserves. But if the kitchen is small, it will be precisely organized, with a place for everything, and everything in its place. Eating with Virgo will probably be a wholesome *cordon vert* experience: homemade soup, rugged many-grained bread, substantial vegetable main course, home-brewed beer (Virgo is rather good at this), unpretentious *vin du pays* or pure mineral water. Virgoan cooks are often inspired, but anxiety sometimes robs their cuisine of spontaneity: they are capable of fretting about the number of salt grains there should be in a pinch.

Eating out is rather a trial for Virgoans; they don't like waste and extravagance and cannot see the point of paying for ambience and the company of others. They rely on places they know well, whose food does not upset their digestion, preferring unpretentious vegetarian cafés or ethnic restaurants with a strong traditional vegetarian bias.

A HEAVENLY HERBAL

Herbs and the heavens have been linked forever; for many centuries, herbs were the only medicine, and the gathering and application of them were guided by the planets. Doctors would learn the rudiments of astrology as a matter of course – Hippocrates claimed that 'a physician without a knowledge of astrology had no right to call himself a physician'.

Healing plants and their ruling planets were often linked via the elements, fire, water, air and earth: Mars, for example, a hot fiery planet, self-evidently rules over hot, fiery plants such as mustard. Herbs that cure the ills of particular parts of the body are ruled by the planet that governs that part of the body. Plants are also assigned according to what they look like. For example, walnuts, which look like tiny models of the brain, are ruled by Mercury, the planet which rules the brain.

All herbs are more effective if they are gathered on a day ruled by their patron planet, especially at dawn, when they are fat with sap drawn up by the beams of the Moon, or at dusk, after a day basking in the strengthening rays of the Sun.

Virgo is without doubt the zodiac's herbalist. The Virgo herbal is extensive, covering many blue- and yellow-flowered herbs, all of them known from ancient times for their many healing properties, with the emphasis on the digestive, respiratory and nervous systems. The long list includes aniseed, caraway, dill, hyssop, camomile, myrtle, tansy, and haresfoot.

Strong tasting aniseed is an established remedy for hiccups and flatulence and is still used to make cough remedies. Hyssop is a venerably ancient cure for asthma, lung infection, chronic catarrh and its attendant queasiness. Dill has many properties, but is most famous for its brisk effectiveness on infant colic and wind. The essential oil pressed from dill seeds provides the active ingredient in babies' gripewater; and the leaves make an excellent disinfectant, very satisfactory to fastidious Virgo. Caraway offers another cure for colic and wind, and contains lots of phosphorous, excellent fuel for the brain. Camomile flowers produce a gentle infusion to soothe stomach troubles; used as a face and hair wash it preserves a pale complexion and blonde colouring.

V I R G O
THE CELESTIAL BODY

 ach part of the body comes under the influence of a different zodiac sign. Disciplined, hardworking Virgo rules the body's two great processing systems, the intestines and the nervous system. The intestines are a systems analyst's dream, an infinitely complex maze of tubes that collects, selects, directs or rejects the food that comes from the stomach. Its success (and our good health) depends on precise analysis, the ability to separate the good and useful from the bad and positively harmful. While the intestines process material, the nervous system deals with data, analysing and collating all the information assembled by the body's sense organs.

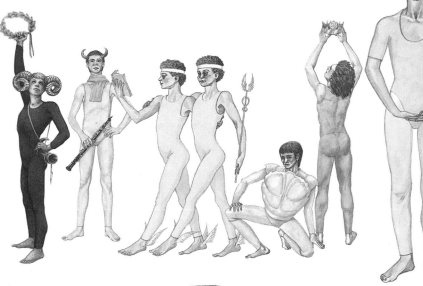

As the part of the body ruled by the polar sign often causes health problems, Virgo may suffer from troublesome feet, which are ruled by Pisces. Mercury, Virgo's ruler, is associated with the lungs and respiratory system and the brain and nervous system.

Virgos are very prone to digestive problems: they are professional worriers and this may show up in indigestion, ulcers or other intestinal disorders. Careful balancing of the diet, together with regular relaxation will help combat this. Rosemary tea (drunk cool) soothes nervous indigestion; yoga and meditation techniques will help relaxation. Exercise also calms the nerves, and Virgos have the application and self-discipline to become top-flight gymnasts or ballet dancers. After a hard day organizing the world, Virgo should float away anxieties in a warm bath laced with soothing oils such as basil, bergamot and vetivert.

THE STARS AND THE STONES

unes are a code, secret keys to the different facets of the whole interconnecting universe. Originated by the Germanic nomads who wandered the plains of northern Italy some 500 years before Christ, this compact and portable form of magic crossed the Alps and spread throughout northern Europe and Scandinavia. The twenty-four 'letters' of the *futharc* (an acronym of the first six letters of the runic alphabet) were used by the pragmatic Germans as a straightforward recording medium, as well as a shortcut to tapping the secrets of the universe. Each rune is a powerpacked symbol of one aspect of existence – for example, the fourth rune *As* means ash tree, but also signifies the tree of the world, the divine force that controls the cosmic order.

When the runes are cast, they combine, and the trained runemaster can read what has been, what is, and what influences are shaping future events. Authentic ancient runes, the portable arkana, were carved or painted on fresh-cut fruitwood and cast onto a white cloth for divination, but pebble or stone runes work just as well. Everyone should make their own runes – they have personal power, and they are free.

Runic astrology divides the sky into twenty-four segments, or seles, which correspond with the futharc. The seles modify the expression of planetary energy as each planet passes through them. The planets carry the attributes of the northern gods, and these too have runic associations.

As the sun signs do not coincide with the runic seles, they often come under the influence of two or more runes. The Virgo runes are *As, Rad* and *Ken. As,* Odin's rune, represents the sacred ash tree considered to be the cosmic axis of the runic world, just as Mercury's serpent-twined caduceus was considered the axis of the classical world. *As* signifies correct order and stability. *Rad*, the wheel, transports and transforms, relying on every working part to pull together to achieve a common purpose. *Ken*, a flaming torch, transforms by illumination, signifying intellectual enlightenment, understanding of the theory of organization and systems. The runic image of Virgo, the hands-on transformer, intellectually and physically concerned with organizing the world, translating formless chaos into fruitful order, bringing every component to work together, is remarkably similar to the zodiacal profile.

Odal, As and *Gyfu* form the trio of runes associated with Virgo's ruler Mercury, whose northern equivalent is Odin, the god of wisdom who snatched the secret of the runes from the world tree Yggdrasil. *Odal*, meaning homeland, represents community, native intelligence and resourcefulness, inherited folk wisdom. *As*, the ash tree, also means god, specifically Odin; and *Gyfu*, meaning gift or talent, embraces the Virgoan imperative of sharing and interchange.

ZODIAC TREASURE

he zodiac treasure hoard may overflow with gorgeous gems, but it is guarded by grumpy and confused dragons, who squabble among themselves and cannot agree on which stone best fits which sign. However, the beguiling idea of a jewelled girdle encircling the zodiac is an ancient one, and may even be based on the twelve

gemstones, one for each of the tribes of Israel, set on the breastplate of the Jewish high-priests of biblical times. Medieval astrologers felt reasonably sure of their ground and listed the gems as follows, in zodiacal order: bloodstone, sapphire, agate, emerald, onyx, carnelian, chrysolite, aquamarine, topaz, ruby, garnet and amethyst. Catherine de Medici, the original power-dresser, was rumoured to possess a glittering belt of zodiacal gems.

As there is no real concensus in the matter, a new approach is needed. Consideration of the colour and characteristics traditionally attributed to each sun sign may lead to a satisfying match of sign with stone.

Virgo's colours are rather restrained and reticent; decorous madonna blue, dark leaf green, autumnal brown, sober greys – the colours of working clothes. Not a very encouraging palette for the jeweller to match, but perseverance brings its reward: consider the soothing blend of olive and leaf colours in moss agate, an excellent stone to calm Virgoan anxiety. The buff and ivory layers of sardonyx also suit Virgo's discreet sobriety; this is the stone used to make intricate and detailed cameos.

Practical Virgo might like to combine crystal power with self-ornament, but would have to be wealthy: jade and rubies don't come cheap. Gemstones apart, it is intricacy and detail that fascinate Virgo above all – delicately plaited and woven chains, complicated rings that come apart like Chinese puzzles. Virgoans also adore those old-fashioned chains or rings set with tiny gemstones whose initials spell out their name or a touching sentiment – a bracelet strung with a minuscule diamond, emerald, amethyst, ruby, emerald, sapphire and turquoise would be prized as much for its intriguing qualities (check the initial letters) as for its mineral content. When buying jewellery for Virgo, remember that Virgoans don't appreciate extravagance, which they perceive as waste; the comforting repeat pattern of a string of delicately carved or painted beads, especially if hand-crafted, will please more than a fistful of bright rocks.

V I R G O
EARTH'S HIDDEN POWER

eneath the earth, in the realm of Pluto, lie the solidified energies, metals and crystals that hum with compacted potency. Virgo's metal is mercury, otherwise known as quicksilver, the mobile silver-white metal that is never still, moving and flowing incessantly, scattering into heavy little globules and recoagulating before your very eyes. Mercury responds so quickly to its environment that it can accurately measure minute changes in temperature. It is also extremely poisonous.

Consequently it is difficult, not to say downright dangerous, for Virgos to fill their homes with their native metal. Practical Virgo may substitute nickel silver for mercury – it is rust-resistant and polishes to a high-gloss shine. However, as Virgos love collecting and classifying, they might make an attractive collection of antique medical thermometers, especially if these were displayed with other (tasteful) medical bygones; think how blissfully satisfying to the Virgoan soul to discover an old apothecary's cabinet – all those tiny drawers and precision-made compartments.

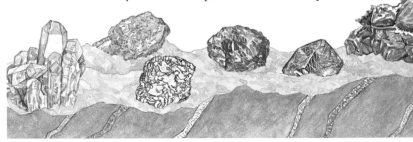

Crystals are chemical elements compressed over millenia into dense, solid form, storehouses of electromagnetic energy. Virgo wheels out some pretty heavy crystal artillery. Remember that the twisted serpents on the symbolic staff of Mercury, Virgo's ruler, represent the inextricable strands of good and evil that bind humanity. Those who recognize and properly evaluate the power of evil and daily contemplate the fact that good's triumph is never permanent need protection to prevent their spirits from fragmenting under the strain. Carnelian, a very tough variety of chalcedony, offers a high level of psychic protection, promotes courage and energizes on physical, spiritual and emotional levels. A second line of defence is offered by the ruby, the Sun's crystal (Mercury can occasionally borrow some strength from its giant neighbour), which is a powerful all-over healer for both body and mind. Cool green jade encourages clarity of mind, purity of thought, justice and modesty. And modest moss agate fosters long life, calms Virgoan anxieties and promotes strength of mind.

Virgo's ruler, Mercury, also opts for agate, specifically the dual crystal, white and amber agate. The intermingled stripes mix the soothing, strengthening qualities of cool white agate with the properties of warm yellow amber, which activates the intellect.

VIRGO ON THE CARDS

 ometimes called the Devil's Picture Book, the tarot was probably created in the twelfth century, but its origins are suitably shrouded in secrecy. There are seventy-eight cards: twenty-two in the Major Arcana, a gallery of enigmatic archetypal images from the Fool via the Wheel of Fortune to the World; and fifty-six in the Minor Arcana, divided into four suits – coins, cups, swords and batons (or wands).

Tarot cards, being one of the ways to explore the human psyche, have an affinity with the zodiac sun signs, and both cards from the Major Arcana, and the court cards from the Minor Arcana are associated with specific signs and their ruling planets. When a sign is represented by two or more cards, they should be considered together.

Virgo has two powerful representatives in the Major Arcana, The Popess or High Priestess, and Temperance. The Popess, the second card in the Major Arcana, is the wise, inspired woman, shown studying a great tome, the gatherer, analyser and translator of information. Discreet and discriminating, she has great occult powers and is the *châtelaine* of the keys to the hidden mysteries of existence. She is closely associated with Hera, the powerful consort of Zeus, the symbol of the *anima*, the feminine principle. Too close a study of life's mysteries can sour the good Popess into a wicked sorceress.

Temperance, another strong feminine principle, is the fourteenth card in the Major Arcana; she symbolizes moderation, the careful, diligent blending of life's elements in their correct proportions, discipline, foresight and control. Temperance must be careful not to let obsession with narrow rules and systems restrict the creative flow.

The Virgoan representative in the Minor Arcana is the Queen of Swords, a stern, bright-eyed monarch with a rapier wit and a mind like a steel trap. Intelligent and resourceful, she is prone to nag and nit-pick, and her barbs of malicious gossip can pierce others to the quick.

Virgo's ruler Mercury is associated with the Magician, a very powerful complex figure, the second card in the Major Arcana, but assigned the number one as the Fool, the first card, has no number. He controls the whole of the Minor Arcana – his stage props are miniature cups, balls, sticks and a small sword – and his distinctive hat, shaped like a lateral figure of eight, symbolizes his allegiance to Hermes (Mercury), whose sacred occult number is eight. The Magician is intelligent, versatile, flexible, clever, dextrous and manipulative, fascinated by the many possible paths to wisdom. The downside of the Magician is the juggler, the smart, tricksy deceiver.

INDEX